DREAM HOUSE

DREAM HOUSE

NIGHTWOOD EDITIONS

2023

a poem

CATHY STONEHOUSE

Nightwood Editions
P.O. Box 1779
Gibsons, BC V0N 1V0
Canada
www.nightwoodeditions.com

COVER PHOTO by Iohannes Soute
COVER AND TEXT DESIGN: Libris Simas Ferraz / Onça Design

Nightwood Editions acknowledges the support of the Canada Council for the Arts, the Government of Canada, and the Province of British Columbia through the BC Arts Council.

This book has been printed on 100% post-consumer recycled paper.

Printed and bound in Canada.

LIBRARY AND ARCHIVES CANADA CATALOGUING IN PUBLICATION
Title: Dream house / Cathy Stonehouse.
Names: Stonehouse, Cathy, author.
Identifiers: Canadiana (print) 20230444342 | Canadiana (ebook) 20230444369 |
    ISBN 9780889714625 (softcover) | ISBN 9780889714632 (EPUB)
Subjects: LCGFT: Poetry.
Classification: LCC PS8587.T674 D74 2023 | DDC C811/.54—dc23

For Madeline Jean (1932–2021) & Freya Alice

A creature that hides and "withdraws into
its shell," is preparing a "way out."
— GASTON BACHELARD

Contents

DOREEN AVENUE—
soft rooks, ceramic dogs in the windows,
the burnt-dust, World-War-II rattle
of a sleep-smeared #91 bus

one turn, another and then
another into the eerie greenness
of a cul-de-sac

hanging basket, four-digit key code,
cry for help, daytime TV,
smell of lost worlds

melting
into their simplest elements:
your brief signature
pressed

into this perfectly bound
visitors' book,

sugar, phosphates, gold
rings, surnames, breath—

I

THE LONG
ROOMS

In the home that is not her home
your mother has draped herself
in a "Flowers of the Cotswolds"
tea towel, behind which
white-boned birds
rise from the clifftops
of her marriage to a psychopath.

Outside, museum leaflets
flutter past, Costa Coffee lids; flamingos
and vultures drift along silent corridors.

Inside, your mother closes her blue eyes on the future.
Custard congeals into yellow pellets
while nurses offer ointment
to smear on her lesions—
the wrong sort.

Inside, there are long rooms—
empty, full of the shells of older women.
Girls in leather sandals, running
for the tram. A gloved hand, attached
to a mask, which isn't for her,
but passes through her
like a memory of the sun
or a man, dancing on a restaurant table.

Inside, there are rooms
overlooking High Street, where your mother
has seated herself at a grimy window,
ready to perform for the stalled
passengers: a scene from *Hay Fever*.
Her black nylon negligee
tied with a scarlet cummerbund.
Someday soon, someone will recognize
her potential and upgrade her cabin
to one with a view of the sea. A round window
through which rafts of migrants
might be visible.

There are no doorways
into the long rooms. They echo
instead with the rattle of distant theme
tunes. A pair of kitchen curtains
sewn into a bloodless grandmother. Delia Smith's
recipe for risotto verde. Hallways that connect
arm to body, soul to head.

In those days, the boys played tennis
while I sat quietly beside Mother
and Father slept
beneath his horse
on the Southern Frontier

we all ran through the emptied rooms
when the adults went drinking,
tried out voices until one spoke,
projected me all the way into
John Carpenter Street

I was everyone then
Antigone Rosalind Sonya Abigail
one skirt on, one in the wash

then the letter arrived
just after I'd left, returned
to our one room
to take my turn
sleeping beside the closed piano:

that bright voice we couldn't get rid of

Mother kept her saucepans on its lid

II

A RECIPE FOR TRIFLE

IN THE DOORWAY of her council house
your grandmother pins flowers to her sunhat,
dons cracked white-painted shoes
and a nice grey mac
to wear on her walk up the hill—

so very invigorating
she returns years after she leaves,
a crusted milk pan empty
beside ant-ridden sugar, an only twice-used
teabag drying on the radiator, back door
open to a waist-high
forest of weeds.

How close the world feels,
and yet it lags so far behind—
that lone boy's voice rising between stone pillars,
one long, last breath, then another, no pause between.

Your grandmother crochets parachutes
in the sitting room, where two dead sons
and a sister smile down from
the mantelpiece. In her apron pocket,
that one she wore at the café
the day you met,
a recipe for trifle:

whipping cream, glacé cherries
sliced bananas, sherry and ratafia biscuits.
A small room with a narrow bed
in which an angel presses ice to its forehead.
A dining set rotting beneath tarpaulin
and so many whispering nettles alive
in the shadows, it's as if she has turned on the radio:
"And Her Mother Came Too," by Ivor Novello—

then a long sweep back, like a river
of grain in reverse: almost threshing time
and the men walk out
in a line, toward the sunset.
Almost threshing time, and the women
run their fingers over the stoneware,
each lip of pure cold, over which cider comes

III

DREAM HOUSE

OPEN THE DOOR, cross the threshold. Stairs rise up
like tides. Drowned songs sway
across the landing. Down here, your abandoned skin
still breathes: an unseen spider
quivering on a web. You are home; you are not at home.
A plant which is not alive, a wildflower trapped in a frame.

What is the price of this cocoon? How may it be
dismantled? Its eggs dead; its larvae
desiccated into paper models.
This is how life was once lived.
A room full of women
weaving lies into capes. A mechanical contraption
for slicing eggs. The rudiments
of interspecies conception
unwinding inside a battered Sony cassette deck.
Your old thoughts, laid end to end
along the skirting boards, eaten into
by ants and ghosts

To go home is no longer possible.

The church you prayed in, playground you swung in, prison you broke from

lie empty, converted anachronisms.

By taking off your fingers, open the lock.

Maple syrup cookies, Scottie Dog shortbreads. Shit-stained tiles.

Touch nothing; inhale nothing.

To go home, unzip the mouth of your suitcase. A flaming pair of gloves

flies out

Open the door, cross the threshold. There is
the ceramic hen, the metal teapot. There is
the Assault Commemorative Plate, with its delicate motif
of intertwined forget-me-nots, mounted against the wall. There is
the green-upholstered, mid-century armchair
under which you smeared excess snot. There is
the bloodstained bed, the dog with one eye, the field
where you split in two.

No one has yet put a hotel on Park Lane.
The knives and forks have their own secret door
into the kitchen. And there is the wallpaper, peopled
by mermaids, some of whom have since become
famous: David Bowie, Princess Margaret.
When you raise it, the roof comes away in your hands

Their dream house floats. Their dream, small as the tip
on a snail's horn. Set well back from social norms, on a service road
with trees and a green embankment to the front, this extended
three-bedroom semi-detached property, which needs a little
updating, offers spacious neglect and stunted moral stature
along with single garage and long driveway. A mollusk of hope, positioned
on a nub of earwax. Viewing is a must, to appreciate the claw marks within

Inside you, there is the Pacific Ocean. There is also
the Andromeda Galaxy, a strange ring galaxy and a Small
Magellanic Cloud. Below them there is fresh air
and the constant relief of not being confined. Inside you,
an empty coracle sits on a bed of moss. Beside it
a sheep crops turf, while in the background can be heard
yodelling. Inside, caribou migrate for weeks across a tundra
which stares up at the dark side of the moon. Inside there is
the hole, up which the poet places her hand.
What are you doing? it asks.
Can a hole talk? Because there are lakes in here
that have never seen bottom, eohippi
that decline to become horses, and janitors
who have never opened a broom closet. Which is a good thing,
because opening broom closets leads to turbulent flow

At school, you were taught the difference
between chalk and cheese. That it was one thing
to scream in a police station, another
to do so in orbit. At school, you were taught
the difference between Cavaliers and Roundheads.
A child with a room inside, seeking a needle.

Because this is how speech exits the body:
in vibrato scratches, when the tree you have hidden in
contains neither kith nor king

The views from trains make you
melancholic, in that sweet way which says: every moment
drenched. Passengers on platforms are Dickensian, in person
obnoxious. That blonde from Australia
who drank Chablis from the bottle, passed it around the carriage—
Come on people, it's Friday!—then talked non-stop
about her HR career. You wanted to eject her, crawl deeper
inside your newspaper, all collar turned up around
your chitinous beetle self. So long as the clouds are moving,
the little churches and burned cars never land.

You detected the ticklish texture of the train seat. Sat
with your knees pressed together, the way your mother
always said you should. Looked left and right, saw snow-frilled
bramble leaves widen, frost crystals soldier along fences
like erect iron filings, and resolved to make love
to the ice maid inside your body—

but then, on the night train, folded your contentious viewpoint
into an envelope. Inside your mind there were others, travelling dark paths
through the canteen, but without clear thoughts.
You were privileged, yet ignorant.
You could spoon lentils into your mouth, but go no further.
Your love was not a metaphysical act

You were the Little People's amanuensis.

At school, you imagined a smaller school, inside yourself, inside which
smaller people would learn how to grow. At school, you built a fence
out of Iron Age swords, at night dismantled it
because otherwise the villagers could not get through.

At school, the desks were snapping hippopotamus mouths.

At school, they floated slowly along the rivers of you, two smiling dolls
in search of a rock to catch on.

At night, you refilled their cartridge pens.

Recalibrated the Fibonacci spirals
of their nautilus shells, cranked them around
another notch or two, just in case there was any further to go

What matters when conjugating absence
is to separate present from past. The first obstacle to eliminate:
her handwritten thesis—its perfect spelling matters not.
Next, pixelated crenellations: her holiday snaps from Spain,
Mallorca, Bermuda, Switzerland and again Spain. Tasting blood, you flick
through her Letts pocket diaries, aged thirteen to eighty-three: exterminate,
    exterminate.
No one can read her copperplate handwriting
and who cares how she felt about the sunset on December 22, 1963.
Next, unfinished paintings—Spanish dancers in acrylics, moored boats
in water—most are bad, and those which are good aren't good enough.
All the brushes, plus the adult diapers, unsent letters
to the County Council, creased-up programs for ballets, and the labelled
    remains
of her final middle-aged love affair which ended in his marriage—to
    someone else.
What matters when transcribing are the elisions...
here is where some words fell out, because they were considered
[by the transcriber]
irrelevant...
...a lock of your baby hair... that fractured clavicle...
her recipe for pineapple upside-down pudding...

In other news, hundreds of bleached-blondes in 1980s track suits
have been condemned to death

There is comfort in the night, which arrives
like a slowly accumulating precipitate, always darkest
nearest the ground. These days
it extinguishes colour quickly, plunges red
like hot glass into black.
After blue, there is no comparison.
You crawl along the landing
in your nightdress, try not to notice the bad breath
of other poets beside you. Stripped of their names, they are
voiceless, secretly relieved

Some mornings you run through the village
until the road ends. The ice from the seventeenth century
never quite melts, attaches to your gloves
in glistening blisters. How are things in Blighty?
You're out of tampons, beyond the reach of Wi-Fi
and the ghosts of Royalists are rising up through the trees.

Remember the little match girl, who stared
through the window? When you closed the curtains her face still hung in
    the air.

Only the river remembers.
First stagecoaches, then steam engines, then Snapchat.
You follow her track through the precinct, return her library books,
try not to look at the mess they made of the post office.

Cromwell said he'd rather have raised sheep

Where are you now, and how do you picture their fortitude?

Scafell Pike circa 1972, a woman in a hot-pink blouse
and a man in beige slacks, carrying on an argument about Schopenhauer.

Their dream was of escape, but they bought a prison, just big enough
to qualify as a marriage. In each window, placed an oil lamp, and at night

glued rustic cottages out of matchsticks: little shrines, while hope
knitted up the dark. And when they died, were only inches

from the perimeter: that line where a lone dog circles, hungry
for body parts. That soft spot under the ear, where kindness collects

There's an easy way and a hard way to clean old silver.
You choose hard, quickly run out of toothpaste, end up crying buckets
over your ready-meal. Slade: "Merry Xmas Everybody"! Undeterred
by your wimple, bend into the dry cold of hoovering.

Winter is by far the oldest season, although spring may come, and with it a
    soft Brexit.
Out in the back, a fox briskly stipples the snow

Dream narratives: the new police procedural.
Every night on the low blue bed
a rhyme scheme enters, marries a dog
to its shadow. Slow dawns, you pull the hands
from your neck, slip deeper
into your standby Other: Justicio Ludovici.
His ripe syllogisms: *A sheep in mitten's clothing.*

Barbara Pym was awfully slim; she wouldn't eat a blessed thing.

A grain of rice, she'd cut with a knife, then eat it with a piece of string

Marmalade, mint sauce, dry
biscuits, Oxo cubes, dark chocolate.

It is a sensible plan
to keep a good variety of
dry stores on hand in the store cupboard

and also a reasonable number
of tinned and packaged foods:
parsley flakes, tinned

peaches, All-Bran, hundreds
and thousands.
This means that a meal

can always be prepared, without trouble,
for the unexpected

guest, or in any emergency
when shopping may be temporarily

impossible

In the mirror, her room bells out behind you, as if there were more carpet
on the other side. A blue Atlantic, over which you step
toward choices lined up on the sill.

Over to the right, her neighbour, smoking Camels in pyjamas;
over to the left, pigtailed tots scootering through Key Stage One.

A pint of milk alone on a path.
Is this her life, or yours?

Low-ceilinged pubs filled with ice
and small change. Disapproving
wood pigeons. The choice between fish pie
with carrots, and fish pie without

Between two and four in the morning, she says,
a dark-haired woman sits on her bed
and aggressively pets her hair.
Ten miles away, down Maggoty Lane

Samuel Johnson the jester climbs up the eaves,
shoots an arrow down, then requests to be buried
where it lands on unconsecrated ground.
Perhaps an old woman who needs a new leg

could steal one of his, he guesses.
Dancing lessons for titled gentry, a stint
on the London stage—all this, then
death, a rewrite citing his life

as a sinful warning. Between two and four
each morning, she says, a stagecoach drives through
her wall. Then a man gets out,
sits on her bed and pulls hard on her hair

There are no new houses. Instead, the derelict cottage
with crumbling lace curtains
refolds itself into a Rubik's Cube of civility:
come in for tea, let's retire to the bed, let me murder you swiftly
over coffee. And each time you pass the cemetery, you see
crumbling apartment blocks, Soviet-style and hissing with samovars.
In Loving Memory of Ruth. May God rest and keep her, along with her
pearl-handled pickle fork. The rowhouses march until they tip over
into pasture. What was it she said? When the new road is built, the old
will rise up to meet it, and the spirits at large in Sainsbury's
gather in the liquor section, whisper *Choose me, choose me*
as you fondle each novelty cider. If you leave as you came, your id
will resemble Maggie Thatcher's, whose hairstyle still beeps.
Unexpected items in baggage area. Moist Brillo pads. Humility.

There are no new houses. Only the dreams of the fields

No angel trumpets, only curlew. February mist, with its damp fleece
of malcontents settling into weed-filled hollows.

To continue north is to risk losing traction, slip down
into unmapped depths, yet to turn back is to betray
memory's Protestants, working their hand looms in cottages made of sin.

Down south there are swallows. Airy cities sculpted
from marble and lime. To continue this line is to collapse
the folds of your compass. Knowledge hangs in the pussy willow, reticent
    with dew

Box up the verses, pocket the chorus.
Shred the curtains, frame the window.
Take the heat from her palm
and press it between two atlases.
Tuck its petals into your jeans pocket.
Carry them in vellum like four-leaf clovers.
Let bad luck be holy for a while

Leaving on the train, you pass yourself
in the corridor, slip into an empty seat, find an unopened packet
of Marmite crisps, continue on your twin paths undeterred.
She detested every cup of tea you delivered. Too strong. Too sweet.
A bubble of grief cruises your entrails. Code words
only say so much, and tranquilizers
are too bloody expensive. If only, she said, you'd married
that mullet-sporting Rothschild. Drink; don't drink.
It's all the same to the multiverse.
John Clare texts: *Get off at Northampton, run naked*
through the butterfly bushes. Leave her remains
on the steps of a Methodist chapel. Carry on
smashing fences, until there's none left

IV

BOXES, NESTS

The House is hidden. It floats. A box of soldiers, a glass-fronted face, a
     curtain
beneath which feet scuffle, each image a darkness
enclosing the house, not disclosing where, when, or for whom it abides.

The house is a cocoon, an open coffin. It is full of weather, and changes
every time you dare to look.

A house at the end of a street, the beginning of something. Numbered
and watched, divided and joined, it pretends to speak, but rocks stop up
     its meaning. Succulents, low shrubs, wilted Laburnum. A brick step,
     sloping drive, a kind of
cramped signature that reveals

how little its writer knows of the language of

ownership. Small objects placed at irregular intervals. A vague colour,
which is not a colour, not even a shade.

The house shrinks from itself. It shivers as flecked wallpaper is pasted on
and pieces of carpet laid down, a red tongue reaching up the stairs
and entering the bathroom. Black and yellow pimpled kitchen vinyl, mute
     white
appliances in which the modern woman prepares hot food.

The house is not yet modern. Nor is it old. It sits upon the clay
like a new idea, a theory requiring wooden boxes in which to think

Why are you staring? Why don't you listen? A body speaks,
mouthless, handless. An open door, questioning what is known.
The fabric of history, worn-out yet tough. A soft furnishing, magnifying
edges:

The cottage is low, its rafters, high. Men in leather jerkins
unlace their leggings in a corner where a fire once burned. Blue cholera
flowers in a winter meadow. Small beer foams from a pewter mug.
Unseen rats bite into quills, wooden cartwheels, rotten hay.

A trencher of stew, a dog at the feet, one hand limning the curve
of a maidservant's rump. A father at the table, polishing his glasses.
A typewriter, an ashtray, a fraying wallet. A mother in clogs, pulling out
sudsy sheets with a pair of tongs.

Birds, now rare, fling themselves like light against a window. An absence
of precision, a dearth of witness. Cardboard library tickets, spiralled
     telephone cords.

Upstairs, a child ("you") stares out of a bathroom mirror, a sheet of
     silver-backed glass,
a reversed window, unaware for a moment of who "she" is, or whose voice
narrates the fate of her shadow.

Soon she will forget and click off the light switch.
The oil lamp, the candle, the dip, the mobile flashlight.

Soon she will forget and open the box again, the box in which this little
     house is kept

45

A father in viscose slacks, drying dishes. A man in loose white underpants.
A white man, with wiry hair in a semi-detached house

who has become someone through privilege or charity;
his own father, the manual worker, placed before ripped gauze
and allowed, momentarily, to peek through.

A brick house, trim painted white. Modest path. Tiny lawn.
The acres of parkland another man might fashion out of bulldozed farms.

This father knows nothing

of the twenty-first century. Instead he faces

out as he polishes this window, small rooms gathered at his back.

Inside, he decides what matters. Small truths, a cigarette's spark, its red rim
nudging the darkness back. The space around him airy
and filled with possessions: women and children, gerbils, negatives,
postage stamps,

lamprey, seal, salmon, porpoises, custard. One thousand two hundred
and forty murdered oxen, eight thousand two hundred dead sheep
and fifty-three wild boar

Are you still here?

        Where did you go?

            Has everything happened?

Stepping into the dark
in an attempt to
find yourself
you do not know if "you"
is in the same room

           When did we speak?

        Is this world now?

Where am I standing?

The house is mute, refuses
to dispense clues. Its walls
layered with newspaper
gaze inward, into the
loupe of an eye
which has never seen.

Is there a clock?

        How many trees?

A man who rode all night
might get here by morning.
A child who draws a blank
might not get here at all.

Either way, the house
remains silent, and wary
its timbers pressed between
storm watch and softened heart

The river is full, almost to the level
of the water mallows. The grass is wet, reddish
clay pools thickening between its clumps.
Calves stand
beside their mothers, whose flat
herbivorous teeth
grind back and forth
like wooden spoons stirring custard.

Blades of shadow
score horizontal runes
in the dull red of cherry bark.
Chaffinches
fuss-budget
between grass and tree branch, tree branch
and open sky

The child in her ignorance is folding boxes, filling them with fly wings and
     paper scraps.
According to the Romans, power is gold leaf, beauty, sun-dried river mud
     and rags.

The Romans built walls. Paraded up and down in ornate sandals woven from
     the skins of
captured Celts. The Celts huddled in hedgerows, wedded field mice, danced
     naked in cloaks
made from caterpillars. When Sunday comes, she will not wear her
     red shoes

It is Monday morning.
She has peeled off the sticker of herself
and stuck it on his camera lens.
Don't look at me. Don't look.
She has taken off her head
tucked it between his shoes
and meanwhile smoke billows out
from the neck
of her dress.

Outdoors, thousands of peasants
in navy blue knickers
harvest sandstone cathedrals
filled with red seeds.

Indoors, a fleet of
sticks clatters over linoleum.
Queen Elizabeth weeps (ever so nimbly).
Out of paper, he has
finished history. Out of broken
alphabets, she fashions
names

By Tuesday, the father's name
            has been deleted

After breath returns, true language
               is no longer spoken

Fox, wolf, deer and boar
pawing at broken concrete
                in a gas station forecourt

An abandoned truck
with its headlights still on
           in the dark

There must be a *something* that belongs in the walls of a poem. A charm or
    curse
made of satin, a dormant egg. Walls are here, as are windows, symbolized
by the dot on the top of each *i*.

The poet wears battered sealskin. She has not been *heron* or *hero*, although
    her
and *he* live together/apart in entangled mutuality beneath stone cavities.
Word-sparks flit through the shadows between their fixed margins.
    Catharsis

does not occur here, only star lives. Sidereal crawl space, who is it
    shines forth—
Celtic kings/queens wearing twisted gold chokers, wild boar
from neurologic forests—1970s shag pile covers them up.

And yet we hear them. This poem

with its open-plan feudalism, anchorites' serving hatches, enclosed
    mytho-commons
punctuated by priest holes,

this poem holds
        many *i i i i i* s

coded into its walls

The robin has a cheerful eye. His feathers hold between them
the air-bones of March, warmth and wind, a scourging sky.
His rust jacket flutters. Pain is about, sings winter robin.
Beware the merry gentleman in his brown tweed thoughts.
The farmer or the blacksmith with rage on his breath.

The wren, the wren. A small brown tailwind on a bicycle. Sprightly, yet
    unsightly.
Up and down the spindrift alley. Lifting her pale, rugged eyebrows.
Spreading the unbroken news.

An unwound wristwatch, egg on a twiggy little bier.

When does spring come, and how will we know when it is here?

This, children, is a poem about British birds and their nests. I have tried
    to tell you
a little about each bird, so that you will know where and how they live;
but the great thing is to know what the bird is when you see it,
and you can only do that by watching and keeping your eyes open

Pavements rise up, glue-glittered with hail
and the pony in the three-cornered meadow
quivers its haunches. Beside the supermarket checkout
lime-yellow daffodils air-kiss from blue plastic buckets
eager to be splayed around living rooms
where women smoke low-tar cigarettes
and dream of French sex.

Soon it will be May, and the screech of new aircraft.
Men in suits flying stunts, hot chrome for miles

This, says Wren, is my future. Everything has been refurbished. Oceans
    swell
outside each window, medicinal plants rustle underfoot. Everything
desirable is hollow. There is no further need for mosquito coils.
All blood sparkles. Everything is pink. Bright at the tip.
Like a pit in which everyone burns their unfinished sentences. That was oral
history. This is narrative. In it, sparrows and stag beetles stagnate, desist

Centuries push quietly between bird bones. Owl pellets
in which an ancestor's body remains articulate.
A bright shoot, snagging the eye of the rabbit catcher
whose aim is to bag a hare before plague grips his throat.
A dwelling at the foot of a bridge
where a woman kneads bread
and imagines walls of sound erected
by her spirit travels. Screeches, mutating into scratches.
A discovery of species unknown to all but the unmedicated
and those who live inside perforated pizza boxes: giant
musical spiders, armchairs with wings

Snowdrops. The reed crosses of Brigid. Green shoots vivid
beneath coats of frost. So much to be heard, almost none of it
audible: the canted stem of the daffodil, creaking upright.
Activist bushtits warbling against white noise.

The man did not live outside history. And yet the house
floats, the house in which he remains hidden. The heather
he once planted continues to bloom.

Inside, the cockroach hums, its warnings of insurrection
not yet outdated. Violets, meadow larks. Horns busting skull plates.
A greening in the cracks between out and in.

No one considers the lambs who died in the fields. Their bruised
afterbirths hang
from the rain clouds at sunset.

This, children, is a poem about insulation. The words
your ancestors gave you permission to speak with; designs
for interiors no longer visible. A suit of armour, worn with its iron
inside. Syllables spliced into hedgerows, between which spirits river-drift.

You must go forth and speak of what you've seen

V

AS OF A HOUSE, WALKING

ALL THAT SUMMER the sun grows larger, trees
thicker, nights brighter, water faster, time
tighter, the air itself
turning from gas to liquid then back again
to solid, a gelid
distillation—dread and desire—

Pressed against the resistant minutes
you push your hands and belly, swollen calves and feet
through each shrinking aperture
to investigate the flexibility of matter, its capacity
to house two separate minds at the same time

Belly ripple, spinal nub, fattened
into a clarifying brilliance:

oil-filled amphoras, anchored in the hulls of moving barges

cheese curds pressed through linen
to filter out what is, from what is not

Hot wasps, agitating around an orange squash bottle. Lips
that itch. The splayed pages of paperbacks. You would think you were home
except you are lost and they have forgotten to look for you,
the ice cream van too far away.

Out in the wood, there's a whisper of ladybirds, their red specks
shiny with private meaning. Out in the wood, the shadows are cool
and the acorns quietly thicken into faces.

Lie down on the rubble of twigs and bracken, imagine your ugliness
troubling the wispy lichen like an anthem sung by dung beetles
and harvestmen. Up there, the serrated edges of sunbeams
ladle light into thirsty chloroplasts, and the dull pattern
of your tank top fades into darkness. Up there, the beginning
of the night is visible as a blue corona around each speckled iris.
Your own face, somehow looking down

In private, when no one is watching, you are nothing.
A flesh balloon, filling up with thoughts.
There is too much within, not enough air, and an urgency
during which nothing happens—like those decades when
only a year passes—this one filled with bombings
you neither see nor hear, the beginnings and ends of lives you never
      agreed to:
George Bush Jr., the children who disappeared on Knowledge Day.
Where does a figure eight begin? How do you step into the stillness of the lazy river?
In private, her neural tube has closed, after picking up the stitches
of older sisters. In public, you wear a green cotton blouse, the shy colour
of early basil. New roses jump at your every step. This is the way, they
      tell you,
out of the ice box. Not the slow dance of fire, but a *coup d'état*

To be an opening through which light comes

To control the angle of this light

To focus its intensity upon her face

To be the matter through which light passes

For there to be no light without this body

To carry around a lens inside the pelvis

Not to see, but to bring forth

what can't be seen

Waking into summer, its livid torches, spiked day lilies, furred spears
of skyrocketing echinacea, you know your undoing requires
commitment, an undressing and undressing
until nothing's left.

There is a seeing which can't be witnessed. A voice, or is that
a face, lit from beyond. It enters in at night, through the gap
between skin and muscle, like a knowing that roots in before.
Some trees have shallow roots, some nights are days, and it is then only
then that you may see her, her translucent body brushing your pelvic floor
with the knowledge that this heaviness will lift.

Stay, says the marigold, lubricated by aphids, don't leave.
Fresh blood thickens the air into storming currents
you must navigate with nothing more than faith.

Already the evening sky has hatched, its blue wings
strung with pyrrhic feathers—cool gravity, drowning you at last

It was possible for him to sleep on his back, unencumbered. It was possible for you to eat rum and raisin ice cream. It was possible for you both to sit between unopened boxes. It was all completely possible in that place of signs and wonders, of grass crackling like brittle in the amber light.

When was the beginning, when the end? To start with, they all wanted to touch you, and that was simply the décor, not the stable walls. Hands offering threats, complementary portions of Thai noodles, the donkey in the background hawing like an old man.

Then the shift, as of a house, walking. Fear in the night, a strained and estranged sense of occasion. *Goodbye*, he said, as you stepped into the bathtub, and in that moment, there was no we

A trout leapt free—

Her body bashes, righteous-shocked, against your blood-strung belly, quiets
into the thrum of time's compression, gravity-pressed, pliable, a soft clock;

the before-time not yet severed but abating, rising
and falling with the pulse in her fontanelle

To be a passage, dangerous and fraught

To be an instrument

of the long dark, closing up now like a sea anemone at the press, its slow
furling inward of mouth, a hidden throat stroked as electric light
touches her irises, their melanosomes still heaven-swept, the brown
not yet separate from the blue

To be a thing and then un-thinged. A false front, crashed through
by demonic wailing. A rag, sodden with fluids, too far in to ever be
pulled out. And what of this could ever be expected—the rage at
cleanliness, the singing shadows, the bone vase full of listening
sunflowers, bending their lives toward the great unheard?

One last cry, and then her face, never before incarnated.

Her envelope, its organ of hope, ripped then razed into an airy nothing.

His yellow shirt, your bloodied hem

lifted to reveal your bodies, zoologic and carnal

What of you can be looked at without looking—the ragged edges
of neglected doorways, your other face, bloodied and torn

swathed in sheets and shame, now its grave stands open
before the miraculous, tender fingers of the obstetric surgeon,
his hair pulled back into a ponytail, stitching you up.

You always close your eyes in photographs. Always look away
from the sun. Prefer
winter, with its flat affect, the cutting edges of bridges
blurred into footpaths

because the light arrives in you
too fast. Her bryht lustre intolerable
without softness, Armstrong's "Melancholy"

palpating the interstellar medium,
her blue, unseeing gaze, its bloodied cap

VI

HYMNAL

TRAVELLING WEST, the elms place their ancient hands upright.
We are not who we say we are, they whisper, and yet the stories they tell are
  mostly true.
Imprints made by the bodies of the sacrificed: leaf mould, hedgehog
spines, the sick heat of curing hay. And when the world quiets, who will
  listen?
A train sketching exits through the foreland, your mind focused
on a single leaf, by which you mean Eurasian wolf, its twilight pressed
against your chest, trying to get out, to get in

The girl sits on the edge of her bed, pulled
simultaneously
forward and back. Who will she be
when she's not where she is? Who
will she meet, still caught in the act?

A bird turns, flies the other way. Already
it has left, or rather, decided.
A change in light, shift in the wind.
Restless agitation at the level of the molecule.

There are those who leave and then return, those who stay
and those who carry on leaving. A yearling swallow
alert to flight, the gathering
and alignment of a richness. A fledgling owl
not ready to hunt, poised
between witness and action.
Beneath them all, horses of smoke,

tiny viral soldiers
carrying pikestaffs

Roads that cross water must be felt, not seen. Far edges hold you in
while you are nothing—neither here nor there, a streak of light

clothed in protofeathers, the odd, striated pelt of a dawn horse.

Keep your mouth closed, lest your tongue dissolve. Everything you know
wrought from spindrift, panic gyres that separate old from new.
Sandstone bays wrecked by the Atlantic, around which roses bloom,
the tent of the self. Slow, ecstatic immersion in the Pacific, its edges
sharpened by theft and razor clams.

An emptiness falls out beneath you, its surface a continuous roil:
shadows netted over by sunlight, the weird innocence
of death by drowning. The blood-boom of surf, a music
knotted out of forgotten bodies

delivered back to the surface

to be counted.

Finding form, even where there is none

Sit down, whispers the Pacific. You are not from here
Stand up, whispers the Atlantic. You are not from here
The house these words grew up in—
no longer visible

On a dark night from the depths of your bed you can hear Captain
    Vancouver's heartbeat
On a clear day from the top of One Tree Hill you can see Boudicca ride her
    wild-scythed
chariot through the Great North Wood

All the goodbyes
and how the voice falters, the singing dream
of breaking into oneself, broken
into words, which approach
then fall away
After the door closes
their footsteps recede, lost lyrics

abrading the page's glass

At first, hymns—

wattle-and-daub

syllabics punctuated by thorn staves—

the ants of the past
      pouring down over your face
                as you open a forgotten window

its furred architecture
                broken/ across
      a 1977 swimming pool sky ...

where falling sparrows
pierce their own   feral vernacular

folios of cloud
      wet-crumple
into blossoms of blackthorn, and Hopkins'

cruciform kestrel

              god-gashes

                        gold-vermilion
the light—

And then that rhyme in which you were held
                    captive to echoes,
caverns of salt opening out from inside:

It, too, a house,
                    where women bedded down on
promises of thistles, warmed their scar-tracked wrists
        at Cock Robin's breast;

it, too, a silence,
                    fractured by frost crystals
unrepeatable as winter shattered
        thought ...

A house unlike
        this shadowy lip
        beneath which Wren stitches
                    sequins

onto pockets

(tiny Lego traumas nested within)

Inside the viol, a sediment of dried-out mouths.
Beside the fire, a mountain of discarded ears.
A tale laid down before you appeared—incest, despair,
a mismatched pair—
and how you learned your part
so well, as if to somehow finish the job,
get it done once and for all.
She wanted applause; you wanted hers
to burn these words
and yet preserve their music and your language.
How to transcribe what was never said?
Draft horses with braided manes.
Her pink linen scarf, well-polished shoes
paintbrush dipped in yellow wood anemone—

You ride your bonny grey mare out into their darkness

ride your bonny grey mare out into their darkness

ride

ride

ride

ride

ride

Notes &
Acknowledgements

I respectfully acknowledge the Musqueam, Squamish and Tsleil-Waututh Nations, on whose unceded lands most of this book was written.

The epigraph is taken from *The Poetics of Space* by Gaston Bachelard, translated by Maria Jolas (Beacon Press, 1964). The line "Winter is by far the oldest season" in the poem "Dream House" (Part III) is adapted from a similar line in *The Poetics of Space*, Chapter 2, "House and Universe."

Some of the language in Part IV is taken from *The First Ladybird Book of British Birds and Their Nests* by Brian Vesey-Fitzgerald (1954): a treasure purchased in Machynlleth, Wales, in the fine company of Helen Pendry.

Some of the language in the poem beginning with the line "Marmalade, mint sauce," in Part III, was found in *Good Housekeeping's Basic Cookery in Pictures* (The National Magazine Co. Ltd., 1958).

Referenced in Part III, Samuel "Maggoty" Johnson (1691–1773), also known as Lord Flame, was an English dramatist.

In the poem beginning "At first, hymns—", the terms "gold-vermilion" and "god-gashes" allude to Gerard Manley Hopkins' magisterial poem "The Windhover."

Cock Robin (the bird) is a figure in British folklore, as in the nursery rhyme "Who Killed Cock Robin?" The Wren is sometimes depicted as Cock Robin's wife, as in "The Marriage of Cock Robin and Jenny Wren" attributed to Robert Burns.

An earlier version of Part III was published in *subTerrain* magazine after winning the 2018 Lush Triumphant Poetry Prize.

Many thanks to the BC Arts Council, whose financial support assisted me in completing an earlier draft of this manuscript.

Deep appreciation to Elizabeth Bachinsky, Sheryda Warrener, Jen Currin and Nicola Harwood, whose editorial feedback was invaluable in helping me see what belonged—and what did not. Many thanks for Paul Vermeersch, Sheryda Warrener and Elizabeth Bachinsky for taking time to write such kind words of recommendation. Gratitude to the P6 poetry group, who first read some of these poems in earlier versions.

Huge thanks to everyone at Nightwood Editions for being so enthusiastic about the manuscript, and for being so great to work with: Silas White, Emma Skagen, Karine Hack and Libris Simas Ferraz.

Love and thanks to Ian for doing this together: building the world, keeping it alive, visiting the home, dismantling the house.

Always-love to W, F & P.

About the Author

CATHY STONEHOUSE (she/they) is a poet, writer, teacher and visual artist. As a young adult, Cathy migrated from Northern England, where she was born, to Vancouver, BC—the unceded traditional territories of the Musqueam, Squamish and Tsleil-Waututh Nations—where she still lives. She is the author of a novel, *The Causes* (Pedlar Press, 2019), a collection of short fiction, *Something About the Animal* (Biblioasis, 2011) and two previous collections of poetry, *Grace Shiver* (Inanna Publications, 2011) and *The Words I Know* (Press Gang, 1994). She also co-edited the anthology *Double Lives: Writing and Motherhood* (McGill-Queen's University Press, 2008), with Fiona Tinwei Lam and Shannon Cowan. She is a previous editor of *EVENT* magazine and currently teaches creative writing and interdisciplinary expressive arts at Kwantlen Polytechnic University in Surrey, BC. Find her online at www.cathystonehouse.com.